FORENSIC ANTHROPOLOGY

WRITTEN BY:
Rebecca Stefoff

mc Marshall Cavendish
Benchmark
New York

All websites were available and accurate when this book was sent to press.

LIBRARY OF CONGRESS CATALOGING-IN-PUBLICATION DATA
Stefoff, Rebecca
Forensic anthropology / Rebecca Stefoff.
p. cm. — (Forensic science investigated)
Includes bibliographical references and index.
ISBN 978-0-7614-4142-7
1. Forensic anthropology. I. Title.
GN69.8.S74 2011   614'.17—dc22
2010010534

EDITOR: Christina Gardeski   PUBLISHER: Michelle Bisson
ART DIRECTOR: Anahid Hamparian   SERIES DESIGNER: Kristen Branch

Photo Research by Lindsay Aveilhe
Cover photo by Hans Strand/CORBIS
The photographs in this book are used with permission and through the courtesy of: Photo Researchers: pp. 4, 7; Andy Morrison/AP Photo: p. 11; Claudia Daut/Reuters: p. 12; Massachusetts Historical Society: p. 19; Chicago Journal, Sept. 23, 1897: p. 21; Harvard Medical Library: p. 24; © Bernard Becker Medical Library, Washington University School of Medicine: p. 26; John Sommers II/Reuters: p. 28; Peter Menzel/Photo Researchers: p. 31; Cristina Pedrazzini/Photo Researchers: p. 32; Mike Appleton/The New York Times: p. 35; Photo Researchers: pp. 37, 42; Jake Norton/Mallory & Irvine/Getty Images: p. 44; Newscom: pp. 46, 50; Mike Kolloffel/Peter Arnold: p. 52; Lexington Herald-Leader, Mark Cornelison/AP Photo: p. 56; Digital Art/Corbis: p. 59; Peter Hilz/Hollandse Hoogte/Redux: p. 64; Reuters/Landov: p. 66; Bettmann/Corbis: p. 69; Bill Greenblatt/Corbis: p. 75; Photo Researchers: pp. 76, 79; EAAF/AFP/Getty Images: p. 81; Getty Images: p. 83.

Cover: Forensic anthropologists, called "bone detectives," often deal with skulls and skeletons.

CONTENTS

Forensic anthropology uses careful measurements and DNA profiles, like the one in the lower right.

WHAT IS
FORENSICS?

AFTER THREE ROCK STARS died in a plane crash, rumors hinted at foul play. Was a gun fired aboard the aircraft? Did one of the rockers survive the crash, only to perish in a frozen field while looking for help? Years later the son of one of the dead men wanted answers to those questions.

Fear and curiosity gripped the city of Albuquerque, New Mexico, after a hiker spotted a jumble of dry bones on a mountain. There was no skull to go with the bones, but a local doctor declared that the ribs and legs were the right size for a twelve year-old girl. Immediately the region hummed with questions: Who was the mystery girl? Had she been murdered? By whom? Law enforcement authorities needed to know whether the bones could reveal who the girl was and how she died.

A horrifying discovery followed the arrest of a serial killer in Poughkeepsie, New York. Hidden in the killer's house, in various stages of decay, police found the remains of eight victims. Five of the bodies had been cut to pieces. Law enforcement authorities as well as the victims' families hoped that individual bones could be correctly matched up with the five skulls. Would this be possible?

The answers in each case came from forensic anthropologists, scientists who have made a special study of the human body. Because they help solve crimes and mysteries by examining skulls and skeletons, these experts are sometimes called "bone detectives." They play an important role in **forensic science**.

Forensic science is the use of scientific methods and tools to investigate crimes and bring suspects to trial. The term "forensic" comes from ancient Rome, where people debated matters of law in a public meeting place called the Forum. The Latin word *forum* gave rise to *forensic*, meaning "relating to courts of law or to public debate."

Today the term "**forensics**" has several meanings. One is the art of speaking in debates, which is why some schools have forensics clubs or teams for students who want to learn debating skills. The best-known

▲ A forensic scientist measures a skull using calipers, a precise tool. Such measurements help the anthropologist determine the gender and age of the dead person, whose identity may be unknown.

meaning of "forensics," though, is crime solving through forensic science.

Fascination with forensics explains the popularity of many TV shows, movies, and books, but crime and science have been linked for a long time. The first science used in criminal investigation was medicine, and one of the earliest reports of forensic medicine comes from ancient Rome. In 44 BCE, the Roman leader Julius Caesar was stabbed to death not far from the Forum. A physician named Antistius examined the body and found that Caesar had received twenty-three stab wounds, but only one wound was fatal.

Antistius had performed one of history's first recorded **postmortem** examinations, in which a physician looks at a body to find out how the person died. But forensics has always had limits. Antistius could point out the chest wound that had killed Caesar, but he could not say who had struck the deadly blow.

Death in its many forms inspired the first forensic manuals. The oldest one was published in China in 1248. Called *Hsi duan yu* (The Washing Away of Wrongs), it tells how the bodies of people who have been strangled differ from drowning victims. When a corpse is recovered from the water, says the manual, officers of the law should examine the tissues and small bones in the neck. Torn tissues and broken bones show that the victim met with foul play before being thrown into the water.

Poison became another landmark in the history of forensics in 1813, when Mathieu Orfila, a professor of medical and forensic chemistry at the University of Paris, published *Traité des poisons* (A Treatise on Poisons). Orfila described the deadly effects of various mineral, vegetable, and animal substances. He laid the foundation of the modern science of **toxicology**, the branch of forensics that deals with poisons, drugs, and their effects on the human body.

As France's most famous expert on poisons, Orfila played a part in an 1840 criminal trial that received wide publicity. A widow named Marie LaFarge was accused of poisoning her husband. Orfila testified that upon examining the man's corpse he had found arsenic in the stomach. LaFarge insisted that she had not fed the arsenic to her husband, and that he must have eaten it while away from home. The court, however, sentenced her to life imprisonment. Pardoned in 1850 after ten years in prison, LaFarge died the next year, claiming innocence to the end.

Cases such as the LaFarge trial highlighted the growing use of medical evidence in criminal investigations and trials. Courts were recognizing other kinds of forensic evidence, too. In 1784 a British murder case had been decided by physical evidence. The torn edge of a piece of newspaper found in the pocket of a suspect named John Toms matched the torn edge of a ball of paper found in the wound of a man who had been killed by a pistol shot to the head (at the time people used rolled pieces of cloth or paper, called wadding, to hold bullets firmly in gun barrels). Toms was declared guilty of murder. In 1835 an officer of Scotland Yard, Britain's famous police division, caught a murderer by using a flaw on the fatal bullet to trace the bullet to its maker. Such cases marked the birth of ballistics, the branch of forensics that deals with firearms and cartridges.

Not all forensic developments involved murder. Science also helped solve crimes such as arson and forgery. By the early nineteenth century, chemists had developed the first tests to identify certain dyes used in ink. Experts could then determine the age and chemical makeup of the ink on documents, such as wills and valuable manuscripts, that were suspected of being fakes.

Forensics started to become a regular part of police work at the end of the nineteenth century, after an Austrian law professor named Hans Gross published a two-volume handbook on the subject in 1893. Gross's book, usually referred to as *Criminal Investigation*, brought together all the many techniques that scientists and law enforcers had developed for examining the physical evidence of crime—bloodstains, bullets, and more. Police departments started using *Criminal Investigation* to train officers. The book entered law school courses as well.

Modern forensics specialists regard Hans Gross as the founder of their profession. Among other contributions, Gross invented the word "**criminalistics**." He used it to refer to the general study of crime or criminals. Today, however, criminalistics has a narrower, more specific meaning. It refers to the study of physical evidence from crime scenes. The study of crime, criminals, and criminal behavior is usually called **criminology**.

Almost every branch of science has been involved in criminal investigations. Meteorologists have testified about the weather on the date of a crime. Botanists have examined tiny specks of pollen from suspects' clothes and named the plants that produced them, which may link a suspect to a crime scene. Dentists have matched bite marks on victim's bodies to the teeth of their killers.

▲ Forensic anthropologist Kathleen Reichs testifies in court as an expert witness.

Anthropologists are scientists who study human beings, past and present. Forensic **anthropology** means applying that particular science to crime investigation. Forensic anthropologists have helped solve thousands of cases around the world. Their main contribution is examining corpses or human remains, usually in skeleton form, in order to identify them. During such an examination, the anthropologist may also find evidence of when the person died, or how.

Forensic anthropologists have solved historical puzzles and modern mysteries. They have brought peace to grieving families by answering questions about missing people and murder victims, and they have thrown light on long-buried crimes. Through forensic anthropology, bones can tell their stories long after death.

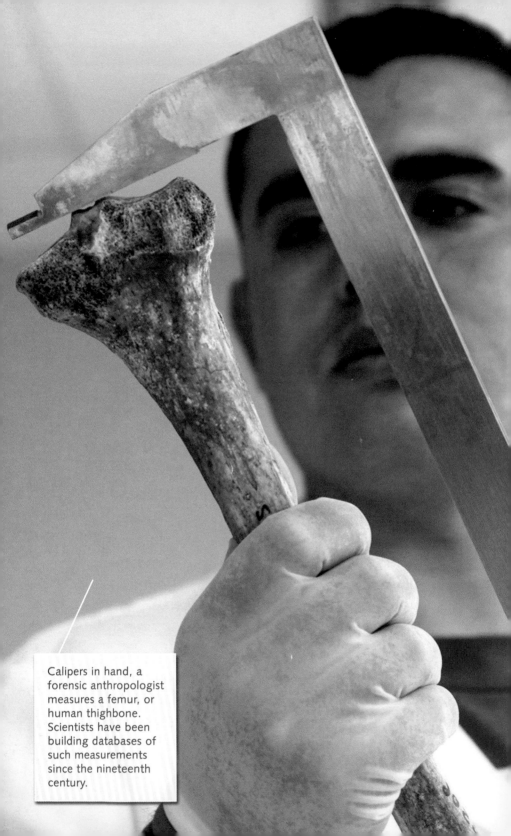

Calipers in hand, a forensic anthropologist measures a femur, or human thighbone. Scientists have been building databases of such measurements since the nineteenth century.

CHAPTER ONE

BONE DETECTIVES

▼ *ANTHROPOLOGY* COMES FROM THE Greek words meaning the science of man, or mankind. It is the scientific study of human beings past and present. Anthropology took shape as a science in the eighteenth and nineteenth centuries, around the time that forensics was becoming a tool in crime solving. Two of the nineteenth century's most notorious murder cases proved that anthropology could help catch criminals, setting the stage for the birth of modern forensic anthropology.

The twentieth century brought new uses for anthropology, such as identifying the remains of soldiers killed in battle. It also brought growing recognition of the ways anthropologists could help investigate crimes and mysteries. By the 1970s anthropology was recognized as a special field within forensic science. Today police and sheriff's departments, the Federal Bureau of Investigation (FBI), and international law enforcement agencies consult regularly with forensic anthropologists.

The work of the bone detectives is gruesome at times, yet it holds a strong fascination for many people. In the popular media, television shows such as *Bones* and *Forensic Files* explore the work of forensic anthropologists. Best-selling books have been written by men and women who solve mysteries by piecing together the tale of the bones.

▶ FOCUSING ON THE BODY

The study of human beings is an enormous subject. To make it simpler, anthropologists divide their subject into two broad categories, physical and cultural.

Physical anthropology, which is also called biological anthropology, is concerned with the human body. Physical anthropologists are interested in human evolution (how our species has changed over time) and human variation (the biological similarities and differences among individuals and groups).

Cultural anthropology examines the nonbiological aspects of human life and society. Cultural anthropologists are interested in such things as languages, the objects people make and the structures they build, and the ways people in different cultures organize their families and communities.

Physical and cultural anthropology are each subdivided into many distinct fields. Here are some of them:

PHYSICAL ANTHROPOLOGY
- Paleoanthropology—the study of fossils of early humans and their ancestors
- Epidemiology—the study of disease and how it affects human populations
- Neuroanthropology—the study of how the human brain evolved over time
- Osteology—the study of the basic human structure: the skeleton and its parts

CULTURAL ANTHROPOLOGY
- Archaeology—the study of past cultures through examination of the remains of buildings and objects
- Ethnology—the study of present-day cultures
- Linguistics—the study of languages
- Ecological anthropology—the study of how cultures interact with their environments

Where does forensic anthropology fit in? Forensic anthropologists are physical or biological anthropologists.

Most of them are specialists in **osteology**, the science that deals with bones and skeletons. This particular type of knowledge can be vital to certain investigations and criminal cases. Forensic anthropology got its start with two of the most sensational murder trials in nineteenth-century America. The key pieces of evidence in each case were skeletal remains.

▶ A DOCTOR DISAPPEARS

George Parkman, a well-known and wealthy member of Boston society, vanished unexpectedly in 1849. Parkman was a doctor who had given Harvard College a piece of land on which to build a medical school. Most of his income, however, came from properties he owned and from the interest he collected on loans he made.

One of those who borrowed money from Parkman was his friend John Webster, a professor of chemistry and mineralogy at Harvard. Over time, tension arose between the two men because of Webster's debt. On November 23 Parkman went to talk to Webster in Webster's laboratory, which was located in the Harvard Medical College, built on land that Parkman had donated.

Webster later said that Parkman's visit had been friendly and that he had paid the money he owed. But Parkman never came home, and no one saw him leave the Medical College. Parkman's family posted signs in the area offering a large reward for information about the missing man's whereabouts or "the discovery of his body."

A week went by, and then a janitor at the college went snooping around Webster's office building. Opening a stone-walled chamber in the basement, beneath Webster's office, the janitor found what looked like the partial remains of a human body. The police came to the scene and searched every inch of Webster's office, finding more remains. In all, the authorities recovered about 150 bones, including some ribs and part of a pelvis. Although they did not find a skull, they did locate a set of false teeth. Like some of the bones, the false teeth showed signs of having been burned.

The authorities believed that they had located the remains of the unfortunate Dr. Parkman. Because they also believed that Webster had killed his colleague, they arrested him and asked a team of medical professors from the university to find out whether the bones were really Parkman's.

Two members of the team were anatomists, doctors or scientists with special knowledge of the structure of the body—its organs and soft tissues as well as its bones. These anatomists placed the recovered bones and bone fragments on a table, arranging them in the proper skeletal order as best they could. After examining the bones, the experts declared that they had come from a man between fifty and sixty years old and 5 feet, 10 inches tall—a description that fit Parkman. Another team member was Nathan Keep, Parkman's dentist. He identified the false teeth found at the Medical College as a set that he had recently made for Parkman. They were clearly recognizable because Parkman had had an oddly shaped jaw.

Webster's murder trial in 1850 filled the headlines of newspapers in Boston and other cities. Curious spectators thronged the courtroom. The testimony given by the anatomists and the dentist made a powerful impression on the jury, which convicted Webster of killing Parkman. Webster was hanged, and the janitor collected the reward offered by the victim's family.

Science received credit for solving the Parkman case, but a few modern researchers have questioned evidence on which the defendant was convicted in the famous trial. In 1850, for example, anatomists did not yet have the data that anthropologists now use to tell a person's gender, age, and height from isolated bones. There is a slim chance that the two men who examined the remains from Webster's lab may have been mistaken when they identified them as Parkman's, or that the dentist was mistaken about the dentures.

▲ John Webster's homicide trial was big news in 1850.

Even if the bones *were* Parkman's, which seems likely, the identification itself did not prove that Webster had killed Parkman. Parkman's family said that the doctor was carrying a large sum of money when he was last seen, and Webster may have killed him and taken the money, as the authorities believed. Another possibility is that the janitor robbed Parkman, killed him, planted the remains in Webster's lab, and came forward with his grisly discovery to claim the reward. Even though we cannot be absolutely certain of John Webster's guilt, the Parkman case remains an early landmark in the forensic use of bones.

▶ DREADFUL DISCOVERIES
AT A SAUSAGE FACTORY

In 1897, less than half a century after Webster's trial, an even more gruesome murder case horrified the city of Chicago and the nation. It started when people began asking where Louisa Luetgert had gone. Her husband, Adolph, first said that she was visiting relatives and then reported her missing.

Police learned from neighbors that the couple had a history of fighting and that Adolph Luetgert had been known to beat his wife. He spent much of his time at a large sausage factory he owned. When the police investigated the sausage factory, they discovered that Luetgert had recently bought large amounts of two chemicals that are not used in making sausage: potash and arsenic. On the night his wife disappeared, he had sent his employees home and was last seen stirring a boiling liquid in a huge cooking kettle. The next morning the floor around the kettle was covered with grease.

▲ Louisa Luetgert's husband cooked up a murder plan.

The investigating officers drained the big kettle. In the slime at its bottom they found a very small bone and a wedding ring bearing the initials L.L. Three more small bones came to light in a pile of ashes outside the factory. The authorities were convinced that Luetgert had murdered his wife and destroyed the body. Chemists confirmed that a boiling mixture of potash and arsenic would dissolve a human body in just a few hours, leaving behind a substance like jelly or grease.

But when Luetgert went on trial for homicide, his lawyer hammered away at the failure of the authorities to produce a body, insisting that there was no proof that Louisa Luetgert had been murdered. The jury could not reach a verdict, so the judge summoned a second jury.

The second trial started well for Luetgert. A medical doctor testified that the four small pieces of bone found at the factory could have come from an animal *or* a human. The state's next witness, however, was George Dorsey, a physical anthropologist from Chicago's highly respected Field Museum of Natural History. Dorsey examined the bones and declared, "In my judgment they belong to one human body." Dorsey's evidence carried weight with the jurors. This time the jury found Luetgert guilty, and he spent the rest of his life in prison.

George Dorsey was the first anthropologist to appear as an expert witness in an American court. His career suffered as a result because his fellow scientists felt he had "lowered" himself by taking part in the scandalous Luetgert case. Yet the second trial of Adolph Luetgert had shown that a trained physical anthropologist—someone who knew a lot about the human skeleton and its variations—could be a forensic resource. Within a few decades other anthropologists would follow Dorsey into the witness box.

▶ THE RISE OF FORENSIC ANTHROPOLOGY

Even before the Luetgert trial, people in law enforcement had recognized the role that physical anthropology and anatomy could play in crime investigation and legal matters. Some anatomists and anthropologists had already provided behind-the-scenes help in such cases. One of them was Thomas Dwight, who has been called the father of American forensic anthropology.

Dwight was an anatomist. In the later part of the nineteenth century he spent years at the Harvard Medical College measuring and comparing human corpses and skeletons. He focused on the skeletal features that differed between men and women, the young and the old, and members of different racial and ethnic groups. Dwight's research showed that a single bone may reveal accurate information about a person's gender, age, height, and health. In 1878 Dwight published a paper about the role that skeletal identification could play in legal cases. His students, including George Dorsey, continued his work of analyzing the human skeleton and applying that knowledge to investigations and trials.

Other pioneers of forensic anthropology worked at the Smithsonian Institution in Washington, D.C. The Smithsonian's National Museum of Natural History had gathered one of the world's largest collections of human skeletons for research purposes. During the

▲ Thomas Dwight was a pioneer in discovering the secrets that bones can reveal.

1930s the FBI, whose headquarters is located near the museum, started asking the Smithsonian's physical anthropologists for help in identifying human remains. In 1939 an article called "Guide to the Identification of Human Skeletal Material" appeared in an FBI journal.

People in other law enforcement agencies read the article, and they began turning to anthropologists at the Smithsonian and elsewhere when they encountered unidentified skeletons or bones.

▶ BRINGING THE WAR DEAD HOME

In 1941 the United States entered World War II, and forensic anthropology soon entered a new era. With U.S. forces fighting in Europe and the Pacific, the army was responsible for repatriating the bodies of fallen Americans, or recovering the bodies and returning them to the United States for burial.

Repatriation was often a difficult task. Few of the bodies recovered from battlefields were whole and undamaged. Sometimes only body parts, bearing no identification, were found. As an additional complication, the bodies of American soldiers were sometimes intermingled with those of soldiers from other nations. The army called on physical anthropologists for aid in identifying the war dead.

One of those anthropologists was Mildred Trotter of Washington University in St. Louis. She ran a repatriation lab in Hawaii, where several thousand American service people were killed by the Japanese attack on the Pearl Harbor naval base in 1941. Trotter and her staff worked to identify nameless bodies by using body measurements, dental X-ray images, medical records of soldiers, and photos provided by soldiers' families. They also made detailed measurements of 790 identified skeletons. This let the scientists link each set of skeletal measurements with a man's known age, height, and race. Anthropologist T. Dale Stewart of the Smithsonian measured hundreds more bones at a repatriation lab in Japan.

The information gathered by Trotter, Stewart, and their colleagues, along with other data collected during

▲ Anatomist and teacher Mildred Trotter worked with the U.S. Army in Hawaii and the Philippines after World War II, helping the military identify the remains of fallen service people.

later wars, revolutionized physical anthropology. Before World War II, the database of information about skeletal remains was small. Most of it came from ancient remains found at archaeological sites or from unidentified bodies. The army's repatriation program, however, produced a mass of data about modern people of known age, race, and height. With a greatly enlarged database of skeletal measurements, anthropologists were better able to identify human remains. Out of the tragedy of war had come a benefit for science and law enforcement.

▶ MODERN FORENSIC ANTHROPOLOGY

Anthropologists had been lending a hand to law enforcement for about a century when, in 1972, the American Academy of Forensic Science formally added physical anthropology to the list of forensic sciences. Five years later a group of specialists in the field founded the American Board of Forensic Anthropology (ABFA) to offer certificates to individuals who have the necessary educational qualifications and pass the ABFA exams.

By that time, research in forensic anthropology had already taken another leap forward, under the guidance of William Bass at the Knoxville campus of the University of Tennessee. In 1971 Bass buried a corpse in a small plot of ground so that he could dig it up later

▲ William Bass surveys a corpse exposed to the weather on the University of Tennessee's Body Farm, where forensic scientists study the process of decomposition.

and examine it. He wanted to study taphonomy, which is the process of physical change in a body after death.

That first experimental burial was the start of what later became the university's Forensic Anthropology Center, also known as the Body Farm, outside Knoxville. Over the years researchers have studied hundreds of corpses—all of them either donated or unclaimed—that have been buried in soils of different kinds, hung from trees, sunk in water, and disposed of in a variety of other ways. By comparing the remains of crime or accident victims with the data collected at the Body Farm, forensic investigators can tell how long a victim has been dead. Similar research facilities now exist or are being built in other locations, to help anthropologists learn how bodies age in various kinds of climates and conditions.

Today forensic anthropologists in many countries are recognized for their services in analyzing skeletal remains and serving as expert witnesses in court. Their role reaches far beyond the criminal case and the courtroom, however. Forensic anthropologists are called upon to solve old mysteries and to probe into the grimmest modern genocides. Whether they are faced with a single bone found in the wilderness or hundreds of bodies resulting from a mass disaster, forensic anthropologists are often the only ones who can give names and faces to the dead.

BECOMING A FORENSIC ANTHROPOLOGIST

BECOMING A BONE DETECTIVE takes dedication, time, and a lot of education. Before you can be a forensic anthropologist, you must become an anthropologist. According to groups such as the American Board of Forensic Anthropologists (ABFA) and the Forensic Anthropology Center of the University of Tennessee, your first step is college, where you will earn a B.A. (bachelor of arts) degree in anthropology. Your undergraduate education should include courses in both cultural and physical anthropology. Biology, anatomy, chemistry, and statistics will also be helpful as you pursue your career.

Once you have your B.A. degree, you will stay in school for another few years to earn a master's degree, or M.A., in anthropology. At this point you have focused on physical or biological anthropology, probably specializing in osteology, the study of the skeleton. You may also take courses in entomology (the study of insects) and odontology (the study of teeth). If your university offers courses in basic forensic science, take some of those as well. Next comes the doctoral degree, or Ph.D., which you will probably need to get a job in the profession. To earn the Ph.D. you will write a long paper called a thesis or perform original research in your chosen specialty.

From your first year of college to your Ph.D., you will spend seven to ten years in school, maybe longer. Even after you leave school, you can take classes, seminars, or training programs to learn new techniques and acquire experience. You may decide to earn a certificate from the ABFA.

TRAINEES AT THE BODY FARM LEARN TO UNCOVER BODIES THAT HAVE BEEN DONATED FOR RESEARCH.

Now you're ready to go to work as a forensic anthropologist—but what does that mean? A few forensic anthropologists work full time for the military or for law enforcement agencies. Most, though, work in universities. Much of their time is spent teaching students or doing research. They work on forensic cases when law enforcement agencies, attorneys, private investigators, or others request their help. Depending upon where the anthropologists live and how well known they are, such requests may be rare. Being a forensic anthropologist isn't always the glamorous job it appears to be on TV and in the movies.

There's something else to consider. Do you have the stomach for the job? The Forensic Anthropology Center warns those who are interested:

> Truly, this work is not for the faint of heart—rotten smells, decomposing flesh, maggots, and body fluids are everyday occurrences, and you will be elbow deep in them. Also, you will run across many sad and disturbing cases that might affect you, so please make sure you are prepared. The good news is, however, that most people who are serious about becoming forensic anthropologists are able to overcome these obstacles.

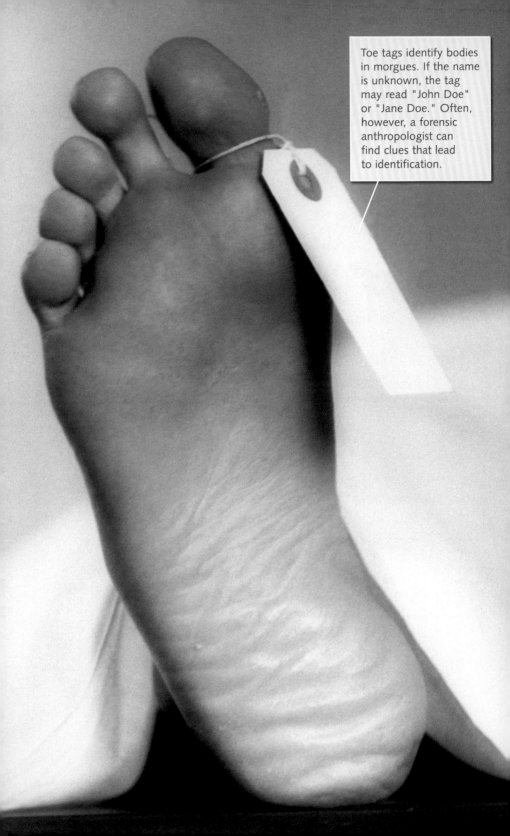

Toe tags identify bodies in morgues. If the name is unknown, the tag may read "John Doe" or "Jane Doe." Often, however, a forensic anthropologist can find clues that lead to identification.

CHAPTER TWO

IDENTITY UNKNOWN

▼ WHEN THE PEOPLE OF ALBUQUERQUE,

New Mexico, thought that a twelve-year-old girl had been murdered and dismembered on a nearby mountain, they flew into a panic. Not until a few days had passed did a forensic anthropologist arrive to examine the victim's bones. He spotted cut marks on the neck bones, which showed that someone had used a knife to remove the head. There were similar marks on the finger bones.

Even more important, the anthropologist saw at once that the mystery bones were not those of a human child. They were the remains of a young bear whose killer had removed its claws. If the skull had been available, no one could have mistaken the remains for human—but certain bear bones look surprisingly like human ones, and without the skull, people had jumped to the wrong conclusion. In this case, forensic anthropology corrected a frightening mistake. In other cases it has answered questions about remains that are unmistakably human.

▶ GETTING STARTED

Forensic anthropologists do not work alone. From the time they are called into a case, they work closely with other medical, legal, and sometimes scientific experts.

When someone who is under a doctor's care dies of illness or disease, the doctor can sign the death certificate. This certificate is a legal document that states the cause of death and must exist before the dead person's remains can be buried or cremated, and his or her estate distributed. But when the cause of death is unknown or suspicious, or when an unidentified body is found, responsibility for determining who the person was and how he or she died is in the hands of a local official—either a **coroner** or a **medical examiner** (**ME**). The difference between the two offices is that a coroner is elected or appointed as a legal authority, but a medical examiner combines legal authority with medical training. Sometimes the ME is a **pathologist**, a doctor who specializes in injury and disease. Pathologists who also have training or experience in determining the cause of death in criminal or legal cases are called forensic pathologists.

MEs and pathologists usually examine bodies of people who have died very recently, or remains that still have some flesh. That is, the ME performs or oversees an **autopsy**, a special medical procedure aimed at finding the cause of death. The first step is to examine and photograph the corpse's clothing and the outside of the body. This part of the process is usually called the postmortem examination and may be performed

▲ Bloody clothing and boots may be evidence of a violent crime. DNA profiles obtained from the blood could lead investigators to a victim, a killer, or both.

by a criminalist or forensic evidence technician and a medical specialist. The next step is the autopsy itself, in which the body is opened and examined for internal evidence of injury or illness. The ME or autopsy team photographs the remains, collects samples of tissues and body fluids, and removes organs such as the lungs and stomach for further study.

Sometimes, though, an ordinary autopsy is useless or impossible. The remains may be badly decomposed, or they may be **skeletonized**, which means that they consist mostly or entirely of bones with little or no skin, muscle, or other soft tissue remaining. Another problem is that forensic specialists often receive only a few body parts or bones, not complete skeletons. Remains found outdoors may have been chewed, taken apart, or carried for some distance by scavenging animals. In cases like these, the police or the ME may ask a forensic anthropologist to perform an examination.

A forensic anthropologist dealing with remains has two goals. One is to provide information that may help to identify the remains, if their identity is unknown. The other is to learn how the person died. The anthropologist may work alongside, or share information with, experts in other forensic sciences. When it comes to the study of skeletons, bones, or decomposed remains, information can come from many sources. A dentist or odontologist may be able to identify a body by its teeth. An entomologist can tell how long a person has been dead by studying insect activity in or around the corpse. A toxicologist looks for evidence of poison or drugs in the remains. A forensic artist can reconstruct a dead person's appearance based on the skull, while a DNA technician can create an individual profile from the genetic material found in the body's fluids, hair, or tissues, including tissue from inside the bones. All these specialists, including the forensic anthropologist, report their findings to the ME or to the law enforcement agency that brought them into the case.

▲ Forensic scientists use the tools of archaeology, such as fine, soft brushes, to uncover buried human remains. The soil around this bone will also be analyzed for clues, such as pollen or hairs.

Ideally the anthropologist will be called to the site where remains have been discovered, so that he or she can oversee the removal of the remains. Anthropologists with training in archaeology are well equipped to recover skeletal material. They know how to make accurate records of the conditions in which the remains are found, such as whether the bones are buried and, if so, how deep. They also know how to handle fragile skeletons or bones without breaking them.

Once the skeletal remains have been recovered and taken to a lab for study, the forensic anthropologist must make sure that samples are collected of everything that remains on the bones—scraps of clothing, plant material, soil, and insects as well as tissue. After that the anthropologist may need to clean the bones. This could include boiling them to remove any remaining dried skin and tissue.

When the bones have been cleaned, the anthropologist is ready to make an inventory, or list, of the remains. This is usually done by laying the bones on a large examining table and arranging them in the correct anatomical relationship to one another, as if they belonged to a complete skeleton.

► TEN QUESTIONS

With the inventory complete, the anthropologist is ready to learn what the remains can reveal. One way to

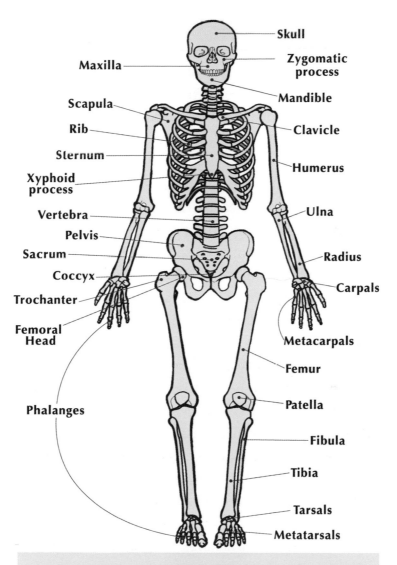

Skull

Zygomatic process

Maxilla

Mandible

Scapula

Rib

Clavicle

Sternum

Humerus

Xyphoid process

Vertebra

Ulna

Pelvis

Sacrum

Coccyx

Radius

Trochanter

Carpals

Femoral Head

Metacarpals

Femur

Phalanges

Patella

Fibula

Tibia

Tarsals

Metatarsals

▲ Bones are the basis of forensic anthropology. The number of bones in the human skeleton varies slightly, because people's bones fuse together in different ways during growth, but the average adult has 206. A forensic anthropologist knows them all, from the largest (the femur) to the smallest (tiny bones in the inner ear).

do this is to ask a series of questions. The answers will build up a profile of the dead person and provide some information about his or her death. Seldom, however, is there enough evidence to answer every question.

HUMAN OR ANIMAL?

The forensic anthropologist's first question is: Are these remains human? Anthropologist Douglas Ubelaker of the Smithsonian Institution has estimated that in 10 to 15 percent of the cases in which the FBI is asked to examine skeletal remains, the bones turn out to be from animals, not humans. Without experience in comparing individual human and animal bones, even physicians can be confused.

When all that remains is a small piece of broken bone, however, it can be hard for a trained forensic anthropologist to know just by looking whether the bone came from a human or an animal. The internal structure of the bone itself may answer the question. The spongy tissue inside bones contains osteons, tiny tunnels through which nerve fibers and blood vessels pass. Viewed under a microscope, the osteons in human and most animal bone tissue are arranged differently.

Those tiny osteons solved the case of a murdered woman whose body was badly decomposed. Police tracked down a suspect and found four small pieces of bone in his car. The suspect claimed that the bone fragments came from a deer he had killed on a hunting trip. Anthropologist Douglas Owsley of the Smithsonian used a microscope to look at bone samples from three sources: the fragments found in the car, the murdered woman, and a dead deer. The osteon pattern of the bone from the car matched the victim, not the deer. When the suspect learned of this result, he confessed that he had killed the woman with a shotgun in his car. The blast had splintered some of her bones, and four fragments had lodged in the car—enough to prove his guilt.

HOW LONG DEAD?

Forensic anthropologists may be called upon to examine stray bones or skulls found in out-of-the-way places. Such remains often look old, but the anthropologist must determine just *how* old they are. Color can indicate how long bones have been buried—the darker they are, usually, the older they are. The amount of erosion or wear can indicate how long bones have been lying exposed in the open air.

The site where remains were found is another clue. Bones found in undisturbed soil, in rural settings, or near archaeological sites or historic graveyards may be older than those found on or near the surface in

▲ The first step in studying skeletal remains is to arrange them in anatomical order. The gaping hole in this skull tells of a violent death. DNA from the bones may identify the victim.

built-up areas such as cities. Objects found at the site, such as clothes, shoes, tools, or money, may help date the remains.

Skeletal remains fall into four broad age groups: recent (from the past few years), modern (from the past fifty years), historical (up to five hundred years old), and archaeological (more than five hundred years old). Historical and archaeological remains do not usually receive full forensic examinations unless an anthropologist is researching a historical question. These ancient remains may be reburied in a cemetery or placed in a research facility or museum. In the United States, however, historical or archaeological remains that can be identified as native American are subject to the provisions of the Native American Graves Protection and Repatriation Act (NAGPRA) of 1990 and must be given to the tribe of origin, or to the nearest tribe if the tribe of origin is unknown.

If remains are modern or recent, the forensic examination continues. The law calls for all such remains to be identified, and the cause of death to be discovered, whenever possible.

The forensic anthropologist, perhaps working with other scientists, estimates the **postmortem interval (PMI)**, which is the amount of time that has passed since the person died. The PMI may be days, weeks, months, or years. The most important piece of evidence is the body itself, or as much of it as has been recovered.

Bodies go through a well-known series of stages during **decomposition**, from initial decay to skeletonization. Climate and type of soil have a big effect on the process of decomposition. A body buried in the warm, moist, and acidic soil of a tropical forest, for example, may become a bare skeleton in just a couple of weeks. But the body of George Mallory, who died while climbing Mount Everest in 1924, was very well preserved when it was located seventy-five years later, in 1999. It was lying among rocks high on the mountain in one of the world's

▲ Petrified and frozen, the body of British climber George Mallory lay perfectly preserved for seventy-five years in the extreme climate high on Mount Everest, the world's tallest mountain.

coldest and driest climates. A forensic anthropologist who uses decomposition as a guide to the PMI must take the weather and soil conditions into consideration.

The anthropologist may also seek advice from an entomologist who has experience in identifying insects or maggots that feed on the flesh of the dead. If the remains are fairly recent, the insects' developmental stage or their activity will offer another clue to how long ago the person died.

HOW MANY?

The inventory of bones may show that more than one individual is present. This will be clear right away if the remains include more than one skull, or bones from more than two arms or legs. Another sign of multiple bodies is bones of noticeably different sizes, such as large ribs intermingled with small ones. But the examiner faces greater challenges when only broken pieces are available. For example, do the snapped-off upper and lower ends of a right thighbone come from the same bone, or from two different bones—and two different people?

If the number of bones is small, the forensic anthropologist can generally determine whether they represent one person or several people. At a mass grave or disaster site containing a larger number of remains, anthropologists choose a particular type of bone—a left shoulder blade, for example. They then count all the left shoulder blades. The total number of these bones equals the minimum number of individuals in the collection of remains, because each person has only one left shoulder blade. But this method cannot prove that *more* people are not represented in the remains. Arm bones, ribs, pelvises, or thighbones may come from people whose left shoulder blades were not recovered.

▲ In a temporary lab erected at a possible crime scene, a forensic technician sifts stones and soil excavated from the site. This method will reveal even tiny items, such as bone fragments, that might become evidence.

MALE OR FEMALE?

A police detective or FBI agent who is trying to identify a set of human remains needs to know whether the dead person was male or female. When all the flesh has been stripped away, the bones are the only source of information about a person's gender. Fortunately, there are skeletal differences between males and females.

Men's bones are usually—but not always—larger and thicker than women's. The bones of the pelvis are shaped differently. Women's pelvises tend to be wider, providing room for the changes of pregnancy and childbirth. Skulls also reflect gender differences. A skull with a square chin and noticeable bony ridges above the eyes is likely to be male. A female skull typically has a more pointed chin and no ridges above the eyes.

AGE?

Another piece of information that can help identify a dead person is his or her age at the time of death. An anthropologist can estimate how old the person was from the size of the skull and bones, as well as other features. It is best to estimate age after the gender of the dead person has been established, because skeletal development in males and females proceeds at different rates.

With remains of children or young people, age is fairly easy to determine. The size of the bone is one piece of evidence. Other useful clues include the stage of development of the teeth and whether or not bones are fully joined together and hardened.

For people over the age of eighteen, the best indicator of age in both men and women is a part of the skeleton called the pubic symphysis, where the two pubic bones meet in the pelvis. The surface texture of these bones changes over the life of an adult, and the changes take place at a known rate. By examining the pubic symphysis, an anthropologist can arrive at a ten-year age span, such as "between forty and fifty." If the remains don't happen to include the pubic symphysis, the forensic anthropologist may be able to estimate the dead person's age from age-related changes in the ribs or from the bones' overall condition.

HEIGHT?

Like gender and age, height is part of the biological profile that a forensic anthropologist hopes to build up from a set of human remains. A biological profile does not identify a specific individual. Instead, it lists basic physical or biological characteristics in order to narrow the field of possible identities.

Height or stature is fairly easy to measure on a complete skeleton. If a skeleton is incomplete, the anthropologist uses **anthropometry** to calculate the person's overall height. Anthropometry is simply the process of measuring the human body and its parts. Over the years, scientists have made thousands of such measurements, building up a mass of data known as anthropometrics. Among the anthropometric categories used by forensic scientists is the average relation between the size of a person's arm or leg bones and that individual's overall height. The anthropologist can measure an arm or leg bone from a set of remains, then plug the result into a formula that will give the approximate height of the dead man or woman. Because anthropometric data are different for men and women, and also for different decades of life, the anthropologist always tries to establish the dead person's gender and age first.

If there are no complete arm or leg bones among the remains, other anthropometric formulas are used to estimate the length of those bones from broken pieces. An anthropologist can also estimate height by measuring bones from the spine or hands.

RACE OR ANCESTRY?

Race may be part of a biological profile prepared by a forensic anthropologist. Yet race is as much a social idea as a biological identity. Race means different things to different people. As anthropologist Myriam Nafte points out in her book *Flesh and Bone,* some people may be seen as white in one country and culture, black somewhere else, and Hispanic in either place. There is great variation within each racial group, and the mixing of groups by intermarriage blurs the boundaries.

Traditionally, anthropologists divided the human species into three racial categories: Negroid (Africans), Caucasoid (Europeans), and Mongoloid (Asians and native Americans). Some anthropologists today regard native Americans, the Polynesians of the Pacific, and the native people of Australia and the nearby islands as categories on their own.

Most of the physical features that we notice in living people of different racial groups, such as skin color and type of hair, disappear when a person is reduced to bones. Still, a few features of the skull can indicate race, or ancestry. High cheekbones often indicate Asian or native American ancestry, for example, while a broad opening for the nose is most often seen in people of African descent. If such clues are strongly marked on a particular skull, an anthropologist can make an educated guess about the person's ancestry.

IDENTIFYING FEATURES?

Sometimes bones have evidence that can narrow the field of possibilities still further. Forensic anthropologists look for marks on bones that are signs of medical conditions or injuries during life.

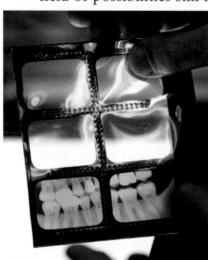

▲ X rays from dentists' files have identified thousands of crime and disaster victims.

Diseases such as osteoporosis or severe infection, as well as injuries such as broken bones and skull fractures, leave evidence on bone. Also clearly visible after death are amputation (the loss of a limb) and bone deformities, such as a curved spine or short leg. Skeletal remains may contain evidence of surgery, such as metal pins, plates, or artificial knee or hip joints. Dental work, including fillings, bridges, and artificial teeth, is another aid to identification.

All this medical and dental evidence can be compared with the medical and dental records of missing people who fit the biological profile. Radiographs or X rays taken during life are especially helpful. With X rays, an anthropologist can compare the skeletal remains to detailed images of a known individual's bones, teeth, or skull. Because there are often small, individual variations in bone shape and size, a close match between an X-ray image and the remains is considered a definite, or positive, identification.

CAUSE OF DEATH?

Whether a dead person's identity is known or unknown, investigators want to know how the person died. The "cause of death" is just what it sounds like—the event or condition that made someone die. Many causes of death do not show up in skeletal remains. For example, a bone detective will not find evidence of drowning or of any cancer other than bone cancer. But violent injuries, or traumas, often damage bone. Forensic anthropologists are trained to recognize the signs of trauma left on bones and skulls by bullets, knives, axes, and blunt objects such as rocks and baseball bats.

The presence of trauma does not necessarily mean that the traumatic violence was the cause of death. An anthropologist can see from a snapped neck bone that a person's neck was broken, but that does not mean that death was due to the broken neck. Suppose, for example, that a woman has a fatal heart attack while hiking. Her body falls over a cliff, and her neck breaks. If her body is not discovered until it has become skeletonized, however, an anthropologist or pathologist will not know that death had already occurred when the neck was broken. In the same way, a knife

▲ A forensic anthropologist studies an X ray of someone killed during Guatemala's civil war, then buried in a mass grave. The fatal bullet is lodged in the victim's cranium.

wound can kill by fatally damaging a blood vessel or a major organ; but if the blade happens not to strike a bone, it will leave no trace on the skeleton.

It is the job of the forensic anthropologist to find out everything the bones can reveal about trauma to the body, and also to rule out conclusions for which there is not enough evidence. Working with other investigators as needed, the anthropologist pieces together the sequence of events before, during, and after death as accurately as possible, based on the evidence.

MANNER OF DEATH?

Manner of death is not the same thing as cause of death. Manner of death is a legal term, and there are only five possibilities: natural causes, accident, suicide, homicide, and unknown. It is the responsibility of a coroner or medical examiner to weigh all available evidence about the cause of death—including the results of a forensic anthropologist's exam, if one has taken place—and then determine the manner of death.

▶ FACIAL RECONSTRUCTION

The German composer Johann Sebastian Bach died in 1750. Nearly a century and a half later, in 1895, two other Germans—a scientist and an artist—tried to reconstruct his face. Anatomist Wilhelm His and sculptor Carl Seffner had an excellent starting point:

Bach's skull. The composer's remains had been uncovered the previous year during remodeling of the church where he was buried.

Wilhelm His was one of a number of anatomists at the time, mostly in Germany, who were studying the relationship between the skull and the facial appearance. Using cadavers, or bodies that had been donated for medical research, the anatomists determined the thickness of the flesh over each part of the skull. This was done by sticking pins into the faces until they struck bone, then marking the pin to measure the depth of the flesh. After gathering many such measurements, anatomists knew the average depth of flesh for each section of the human face. It then became possible for sculptors to recreate a dead person's appearance by molding clay upon the skull (or a model of the skull) according to the anatomists' set of measurements. That is how Bach's face was reconstructed. Wilhelm His provided the anatomical data, and Carl Seffner shaped Bach's face and then painted it. The reconstruction was considered a success because it looked like portraits of the famous composer.

Facial reconstruction is still a combination of science and art. Today it is also one of the forensic anthropologist's most valuable tools for identifying the unknown dead. By showing how a dead person was likely to have looked when alive, a facial reconstruction may trigger a recognition by someone who knew the person.

Three methods exist for reconstructing a face from the underlying skull. They are three-dimensional modeling or sculpture (sometimes called the plastic method), the artist's sketch, and computer modeling. Some anthropologists have both the knowledge and the artistic skill needed to create reconstructions. Often, however, a forensic artist with special knowledge of facial anatomy does the work.

Three-dimensional modeling is similar to the methods used by His and Seffner in the nineteenth century. The process starts with choosing a data set, which is the set of facial measurements that best matches the dead person's biological profile. For example, the average measurements of facial tissue for a ten-year-old girl who is short for her age are not the same as those for a tall fifty-year-old man. Today's facial reconstructors have access to a wide variety of data sets to meet any need. (Medical scanning devices, rather than pins, are now used to measure facial tissues for the data sets, and the measurers use living people rather than cadavers.)

With the data set chosen, the sculptor studies the skull, or a model of it. The next step is cutting rubber pegs to the proper lengths and placing them on the skull at points called landmarks. These are the places

▲ This three-dimensional model of an unidentified John Doe, created by Kentucky forensic anthropologist Emily Craig, may spark recognition when seen on television or the Internet.

where tissue depth is measured for data sets. Next the sculptor applies clay to the skull, building it up to the top of each peg so that the clay matches the data set.

Some sculptors take an anatomical approach, arranging the clay in layers like the underlying muscles of the face. Others simply line up the clay with the pegs. The finished sculpture is painted, then given eyes (usually brown, the most common eye color) and a wig. The result is not expected to look exactly like the living person—there are far too many variations in people's facial tissues for pinpoint accuracy. Sometimes,

▶ THE DNA REVOLUTION

Forensic science gained a powerful new tool in the mid-1980s. A British scientist named Alec Jeffreys was studying deoxyribonucleic acid, or DNA, the genetic material found in all the body's cells. DNA is a set of molecules arranged in two spiral strands that are connected by shorter sections, like the rungs of a ladder. Each rung consists of two molecules and is called a base pair. A gene is the sequence, or series, of base pairs that contains the code for making a specific protein. Within each cell, long strands of genes are packed into bundles called chromosomes.

All human cells share the same basic arrangement of DNA; this is the human genome. For each individual, however, there is a unique arrangement of genes on that genome. For example, the human genome includes instructions for making eyes, but the color of a person's eyes depends on the specific combination of genetic material inherited from both parents. Jeffreys found a way to remove sections of DNA from cells and "map" them, producing a DNA profile that represents a person's distinctive genetic code. This scientific breakthrough was a forensic breakthrough as well, because—as the British police were about to discover—the DNA profile is an extremely accurate form of identification.

Jeffreys's method of DNA mapping was brand new when British police asked the scientist for forensic help

though, a reconstruction turns out to look surprisingly like the original.

The sketch method makes use of the same data about facial tissues that sculptors use. Trained forensic artists can produce sketches of crime suspects based on descriptions by witnesses. The artists use the same skills to draw the faces of the unknown dead, basing their drawings on the features of the skull. An artist may even draw such a sketch on top of an X ray or photo of the skull.

Computer modeling is replacing the sketch method. A number of software programs can produce facial images on the computer screen. Many of these programs start with traditional three-dimensional clay models. The artist makes a model, scans a photo of it into the computer, and uses the software to add the details of the face. Other programs start with X-ray or photographic images of the skulls instead of models. Using a built-in database of features, the artist creates a face over the outlines of the skull by choosing features that fit the chosen data set.

One advantage of computer modeling is that details such as hairstyle and hair and eye color can be changed quickly and easily. The artist can also change other features, perhaps modifying the length of the nose or the fullness of the cheeks. The result may be a set of images, each slightly different from the others, all of them fitting the skull. This increases the chance that one of the images will be a close match to the unknown subject.

FACES
OF DEATH

THE U.S. DEPARTMENT OF JUSTICE estimates that between 15,000 and 40,000 sets of unidentified human remains are stored in coroner's offices and other official sites across the country. That's a lot of unsolved mysteries—and a lot of family members and friends who are still wondering about the fate of someone who disappeared. FACES, the Forensic Anthropology and Computer Enhancement Services laboratory at Louisiana State University in Baton Rouge, wants to do something about it.

At FACES, forensic anthropologists, lab technicians, and computer-imaging experts reconstruct the faces of unidentified remains from all over Louisiana and beyond. Their standard method is to create a clay facial model, scan a photograph of the model into a computer, and use software to fine-tune the image. One old case that has received this treatment at FACES involved the skull of a young man. The skull had been found in 1976, lying on a sandbar in the Red River near the Louisiana city of Shreveport.

In 2007 a sheriff's deputy happened to be in the lab. On a shelf he saw the clay model based on the Shreveport skull. It looked familiar, so he searched through old missing-persons files. The FACES reconstruction turned out to match the description of Victor Barajas, a twenty-year-old Texas man who disappeared near Shreveport in 1976. Barajas's fate had been unknown for

SOME FORENSIC ARTISTS NOW USE COMPUTER SOFTWARE TO DEVELOP A FACIAL RECONSTRUCTION. SOME PROGRAMS START WITH AN X RAY OR PHOTOGRAPH OF THE SKULL, THEN BUILD UP THE FLESH AND FEATURES IN LAYERS.

decades. FACES and a dedicated deputy had restored h name to his remains, and an old missing-persons c was closed.

Thanks to advances in techniques and a gro interest in forensic anthropology, it is becoming to create facial reconstructions. FACES is lea movement to improve the nation's programs for fying the thousands of unknown dead. In Justice Department made a start by launching called the National Missing and Unidentifie System (www.namus.gov). It consists of two One contains information from coroners a examiners about unidentified remains. The of missing persons. Law enforcement ager and the public can search the two data for matches.

They wanted to identify the killer of two young girls. A man named Richard Buckland had confessed to one murder but insisted he was innocent of the other. Police hoped that Jeffreys could prove Buckland's guilt by analyzing traces of the killer that had been found on the two girls' bodies, then comparing the DNA from those samples with Buckland's DNA profile. What happened next made forensic history.

Jeffreys carried out the tests and found that the samples from the two girls matched. Both victims had been killed by the same man. That man, however, was not Richard Buckland. He had confessed to one killing under the pressure of police questioning, but his DNA proved his innocence. Since that time hundreds of people have been exonerated, or proven innocent, by DNA tests.

The girls' killer, however, was still at large. In 1987 the police did something that had never been done before. They asked every man in the district to give a voluntary sample of blood or saliva for DNA testing. More than 4,500 local men were tested, but none of the samples matched the killer. Police then learned that a man named Colin Pitchfork had paid someone else to take a blood test in his name. This made the authorities suspicious. The police requested a new sample from Pitchfork—making certain that it was really his blood—and it matched the samples from the victims. Colin Pitchfork went down in criminal history as the first person to be convicted of murder by his own DNA.

DNA can be obtained from many biological sources, including the roots of hair, skin and tissue cells, blood, saliva, and other body fluids. It is also present in bone tissue. Forensic examiners can get a DNA profile from bones even long after all flesh and soft tissue have disappeared from the remains.

To extract DNA from bones, examiners first clean the bones—with heat, chemicals, or both—to remove surface material that might contaminate the DNA sample. They then drill into the bone to get powder from the internal tissue. Added to a sterile liquid, the powder can be tested for DNA like any other biological material. Using this method, scientists have been able to obtain DNA from very ancient fossil bones, including the remains of long-extinct Neanderthal people. Bones of the recently dead, however, are much easier to analyze.

Bone DNA testing plays an important role in criminal and missing-persons investigations. In 2008, for example, forensic specialists analyzed DNA taken from two bones found in the mountains of the Sierra Nevada in eastern California. Their results solved the mystery of a missing billionaire.

Steve Fossett, who became famous as the first person to fly alone around the world in a hot-air balloon, had disappeared in September 2007 after taking off in a private plane from a Nevada ranch. His flight path appeared to lead into the mountains. Searchers combed the rugged landscape and, after more than a year, located the wreckage of Fossett's plane. Bone fragments found near the plane were thought to be Fossett's remains, until DNA testing revealed that they came from animal bones. Soon, though, searchers found more bones not far from the crash site. Tests showed that DNA from these bones was human and matched the genetic material of the lost adventurer.

Since the Pitchfork case in the 1980s, DNA testing has transformed many aspects of crime investigation and forensic science. DNA can link a suspect with evidence left at the crime scene, or identify a set of human remains. However, a DNA profile from a crime scene or unknown subject is useful only when it can be matched to a known profile. In other words, when an unidentified corpse is found in the woods, getting its DNA profile won't identify the corpse unless that profile is already on file somewhere.

In the United States, laws in various states require that DNA samples be taken from people who are convicted of certain crimes, such as sex offenses, kidnapping, murder, and robbery. The FBI maintains a national database of these profiles. Called the Combined DNA Index System, or CODIS, the database lets investigators search for matches between crime scene evidence and known criminals.

DNA testing is usually done by forensic biologists or specially trained technicians, not by forensic anthropologists. Most tests are performed to confirm or rule out links between crime scenes and suspects. When it comes to identifying unknown remains, DNA can do the job only *if* the person's profile has already been entered into a database such as CODIS. But CODIS includes only a small part of the population. In addition, at any given time there is a large backlog of samples waiting to be tested and profiles waiting to be entered into the system. For these reasons, DNA

▲ DNA samples are prepared for testing at the Netherlands Forensic Institute. DNA profiling is currently the most accurate method of identifying biological evidence.

profiling usually is not the first step toward identifying unknown human remains.

Forensic anthropology, with its system of skeletal analysis, is still the primary tool for identifying human remains. That analysis—or some other police or forensic work in the investigation—may lead to a possible identification of the remains as belonging to a missing individual. At that point, DNA profiling is useful. Experts first obtain a DNA profile from the remains, then compare it with the profile of the missing person. The missing person's DNA profile can be taken from blood relatives of the missing person, or found on objects from which samples of the person's DNA can be retrieved, such as toothbrushes or hairbrushes. If there is a match, the unknown remains are confirmed to be those of the missing person. In this way DNA profiling becomes the final step in the forensic anthropologist's investigation.

HERE RESTS IN
HONORED GLORY
AN AMERICAN
SOLDIER
KNOWN BUT TO GOD

This tomb of the unknown soldier in Arlington National Cemetery held a body that forensic scientists were eventually able to identify as that of a pilot shot down over Vietnam in 1972.

CHAPTER THREE

GRAVE MATTERS

▼ **FEBRUARY 3, 1959, HAS BEEN CALLED**
"the day the music died." Early in the morning of that
winter day, three of America's most popular rock-and-
roll musicians boarded a small airplane in Clear Lake,
Iowa, to fly to the next stop on their tour. Their names
were Buddy Holly, Ritchie Valens, and J. P. Richardson
Jr., known as the Big Bopper.

The plane lifted off and then flew into a low cloud,
an early sign of an unexpected snowstorm. The pilot
failed to answer a radio call, so a few hours later, when
the weather had improved somewhat, another pilot set
out to trace the route of the first plane. He found it

crashed in a field. The pilot and the three passengers were dead. The pilot's body was still in the cockpit. Holly and Valens lay near the wreck. Richardson's body was farther away, on the other side of a fence.

Aviation investigators reviewed the crash site and the plane's instruments. They decided that the crash resulted from mistakes by the pilot, who was not qualified to fly guided only by the plane's instruments, a skill that is essential when a pilot cannot see the ground because of heavy clouds. Not everyone agreed with the investigators' conclusion. The owner of the plane insisted that the pilot understood the plane's instruments and that the sky had been clear at the time the plane went down. He hinted that something must have gone wrong in the aircraft to cause the crash. Such hints were fueled by the discovery of a loaded pistol in the field where the wreckage was found. The gun was Holly's—he carried it in a bag as protection against robbery, because the musicians were often paid in cash. Its presence at the crash site added an air of mystery to the tragedy, and rumors spread that the gun had been fired aboard the plane.

Richardson's son, Jay, was born two months after the crash. As Jay Richardson grew up, he became curious about the father he never met. In particular, he wondered whether there was any chance that his father

▲ A 1959 plane crash killed three rock stars and their pilot. Three bodies, including this victim, were found in or near the plane. Questions hung over the fate of the fourth man, whose body was farther from the crash site.

had been shot on that plane, and whether he had survived the crash and struggled across the fence, only to die while seeking help. In 2006 Richardson contacted forensic anthropologist William Bass, founder of the Body Farm. Richardson asked Bass to look for the answers to those questions in his father's remains.

Criminal charges were not an issue. The younger Richardson simply hoped that the anthropologist would be able to tell him how the Big Bopper had died. After receiving the remains from the Texas cemetery where Richardson was buried, Bass made X-ray images of the dead man's entire body. Upon analyzing these images, Bass was able to answer both Jay Richardson's questions about his father's fate.

If JP Richardson had been shot, lead from the bullet would have left a tell-tale trace in the body, and that trace would be clearly visible as a white streak on the X-ray film. There was no such trace. Bass concluded that the singer had not been shot.

The X rays also showed that the Big Bopper could not have made his way over or through the fence to search for help after the crash. The injuries to his skull, spine, pelvis, chest, and legs were so severe that he would not have been able to move. Bass reported that the singer had probably died almost instantly. Therefore, his body must have been thrown into the next field when the wreckage flew apart.

▶ **UNKNOWN NO LONGER**

In 1970 the Vietnam War was raging in Southeast Asia. Thousands of American soldiers served there. One of them was eighteen-year-old Alan Keith Barton of Michigan, who went missing one night from Camp Radcliff, his military base in Binh Dinh Province. After Barton had been AWOL (absent without leave, or permission) for thirty days, his commanding officer declared the young man a deserter. Barton was never seen again.

In 1982 the U.S. Army was asked to provide the remains of an unknown soldier to be buried in a memorial as a symbol of all those who had died for their country in Vietnam. The soldier had to be someone who had been killed in the Vietnam War, whose remains could not be identified.

The military's Central Identification Laboratory (CIL), which is responsible for the forensic analysis of the remains of members of the U.S. armed forces, reviewed four boxes of unidentified remains believed to come from Americans killed in Vietnam. One box contained a large number of bones, even teeth. They had been found in 1972 at the edge of Camp Radcliff, but they did not match the records of any soldier reported killed or missing in action. CIL's commanding officer did not want those remains to be buried as the unknown soldier. With so much skeletal material,

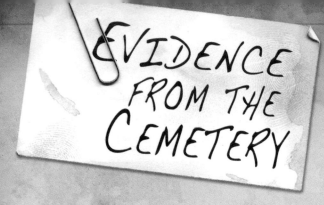

IN ORDER TO X RAY the Big Bopper's remains, William Bass had had to remove them from their burial place. This procedure, called exhumation, is generally supervised by a medical examiner, a pathologist, or a forensic anthropologist.

The investigation requested by young Jay Richardson was unusual. The most common reason for an exhumation is to search for forensic evidence in a criminal investigation. No exhumation, however, can occur without permission. Surviving relatives may authorize the procedure. If there are no known relatives, responsibility for granting permission lies with the court. In cases such as investigating a serial killer or a disease epidemic, the court may overrule a family's objection to an exhumation.

Although it may be hard for family members to think of disturbing a body that has been laid to rest, exhumation can bring to light important evidence in a criminal case. For example, an Illinois man named Drew Peterson came under suspicion after his fourth wife disappeared in 2007. The body of his third wife, who had drowned in a bathtub in 2004, was exhumed for a forensic autopsy. The results led prosecutors to suspect that the third wife had not died by accident. Her death may have been a homicide staged to look like an accident. In 2009 Peterson was arrested and charged with murder. At Peterson's trial, attorneys for the prosecution will produce the evidence from the exhumation that they believe points to homicide.

Peterson's defense attorneys will try to show that there is no clear evidence of homicide.

Exhumation may also allow investigators to use forensic techniques that did not exist when the body was buried. In Colorado in late 2009, the Boulder County Sheriff's Office (BCSO) announced that exhumation had solved a long-standing mystery. More than half a century earlier the body of a murdered young woman had been found. Authorities tried unsuccessfully to learn who she was. Her remains were buried in a local cemetery under the name used for unidentified females: Jane Doe.

In 2004 a local historian wrote about the case, and BCSO reopened it. Investigators obtained a court order authorizing the exhumation of Jane Doe's body, and forensic experts worked with the remains to develop two key pieces of evidence: a model of the victim's face at the time of her death and a DNA profile. The investigation was featured in newspapers and on the television program *America's Most Wanted*. A woman came forward to suggest that the remains might be those of her aunt, Dorothy Gay Howard, who had disappeared from Phoenix, Arizona, in 1954, at the age of eighteen. DNA technicians compared samples from the exhumed body and from a surviving sister of Dorothy Gay Howard. The results showed that both women were daughters of the same mother. Boulder's Jane Doe had a name at last.

Forensic anthropologists are sometimes called on to investigate historical mysteries. William R. Maples, a former president of the American Board of Forensic Anthropology, exhumed the body of President Zachary Taylor, who died in 1850, to see whether Taylor had been poisoned with arsenic. He had not. Returning to the present, forensic anthropologists have provided answers to questions about missing soldiers, crimes against humanity, and grisly homicides.

he thought, the remains should be identifiable. He set out to identify them.

Odontology, one of forensic anthropology's most valuable tools, was the key to identifying the remains. The teeth in the box turned out to match the dental records of Alan Keith Barton. The remains had not been studied earlier with the goal of identifying them because Barton was considered to be a deserter—the army was concerned with identifying soldiers killed on duty or missing in action. Once Barton's remains were identified, however, the army allowed him to be buried with military honors, clearing him of the charge of desertion. A military spokesman said that Barton may have died when he tripped over a land mine at night. It is not clear why his remains were not found at the time of the accident.

A different set of remains was buried in the tomb of the unknown Vietnam soldier, but the bones were not fated to remain there. In 1998 the family of a missing soldier named Michael Blassie learned that CIL had once thought that the "unknown" Vietnam remains might be Blassie's but could not make an identification. At the family's request, the government let forensic anthropologists open the tomb to examine the remains.

Back when the army had labeled the remains unidentifiable, DNA testing was in its infancy. Profiling tests were in general use by forensic scientists in 1998, however, and DNA from the unknown soldier's bones was compared with DNA from Blassie's sister. The amount of shared genetic information proved that the bones were Michael Blassie's. After the remains were returned to the Blassie family for burial, the tomb of the unknown Vietnam soldier was left empty. It now represents the hope that all fallen soldiers will be identified, and none will remain unknown.

▲ The "unknown soldier" turned out to be Air Force pilot Michael Blassie.

▶ CRIMES AGAINST HUMANITY

One of the biggest challenges a forensic anthropologist can face is a scene of mass disaster, inevitably resulting in many deaths. At such times the anthropologist may have to sift through the remains of a large number of victims, identifying each one, if possible, and helping to determine exactly how he or she died. One of the

▲ Forensic anthropology solved a historical mystery in the early 1990s. Scientists proved that recently unearthed remains were members of the former Russian royal family, the Romanovs, who had been murdered in 1918.

modern world's most horrific kinds of large-scale forensic challenge is genocide: mass killing undertaken in a deliberate effort to wipe out a particular group of people.

When Adolf Hitler of Germany tried to exterminate Europe's Jews in the middle of the twentieth century, he was committing genocide, which is considered a crime against humanity and a violation of human rights. Since that time, tragically, other groups around the world have suffered from similar attempts to destroy them. The victims of genocidal attacks and human rights abuses are often buried in unmarked mass graves.

Forensic anthropologists, working with human rights organizations, have investigated a number of crimes against humanity. They search for graves, exhume remains using the techniques developed in archaeological and criminal investigations, and then analyze the remains in order to identify them. Their findings can be vital evidence in the trials of those who ordered and carried out the killings. Equally important, the discovery and identification of remains can bring peace to family members who have lived with uncertainty since the disappearance of a loved one.

American forensic anthropologist Clyde Snow is credited with launching the forensic examination of human rights abuses. In 1984 a human rights organization in the South American nation of Argentina contacted the American Academy for the Advancement of Science, asking for help identifying bodies that had been recovered from mass graves. The remains in question were those of thousands of Argentine citizens who had "disappeared" during the 1970s, killed by government death squads for their opposition to the country's harsh military government and hastily buried.

Snow was one of the American scientists who answered the request. He traveled to Argentina, where he oversaw exhumations and led forensic teams whose

MISSING IN ACTION

FORENSIC ANTHROPOLOGISTS have been recovering and identifying the remains of American military personnel since the middle of the twentieth century. Today that task is overseen by the Joint POW-MIA Accounting Command (JPAC). The military created this unit in 2003 to coordinate efforts to account for all U.S. service people who are listed as missing in action (MIA) or as prisoners of war (POW) as a result of the nation's past conflicts. JPAC is based in Hawaii, and the Central Identification Laboratory (CIL), which was established in the 1970s, is now part of the joint command.

At CIL, forensic anthropologists examine remains that are believed to be those of American service people. Most of the remains come from Southeast Asia, where many soldiers were lost during the Vietnam War years. Bones may come to light accidentally, perhaps found by a farmer in a field, or they may be located by searchers. Such searchers include veterans of the war looking for the remains of fallen comrades, family members of MIAs, and military historians as well as JPAC investigators.

JPAC identifies about six MIAs a month. As of mid-2009 the U.S. government had made more than 1,300 identifications through CIL. However, many more sets of remains, belonging to members of the U.S. armed forces who are presumed dead, still wait to be found and brought home. At any given time, the analysts of JPAC have more than a thousand open files, each representing a military man or woman whose fate is not yet known.

A FORENSIC ODONTOLOGIST AT JPAC
HEADQUARTERS IN HAWAII LISTS TEETH AND
TOOTH FRAGMENTS AMONG A SET OF PARTIAL SKELETAL
REMAINS. IF THE REMAINS ARE THOSE OF AN AMERICAN
MILITARY SERVICE PERSON, DENTAL RECORDS
MAY LEAD TO AN IDENTIFICATION.

members were examining remains. Snow also trained Argentine medical students in the best archaeological and anthropological techniques for recovering bodies and identifying them. He and his students founded the Argentine Forensic Anthropology Team, the world's first organization dedicated to using forensic anthropology to document human rights violations. Since the 1980s the team has worked in many countries, and similar forensic anthropology teams have formed in other nations. The work of these forensic anthropologists has cast light on the horrors of genocide in many parts of the world.

More than 200,000 people are believed to have been massacred in the Central American nation of Guatemala during a thirty-four-year military dictatorship in the late twentieth century. In the Southeast Asian nation of Cambodia, the dictator Pol Pot was responsible for as many as 2 million deaths during the 1970s. In 1994 violence erupted in the African nation of Rwanda when one ethnic group, the Hutus, began slaughtering, another group, the Tutsis. In just a hundred days, some 800,000 Tutsis perished in this violent process known as ethnic cleansing. Most were mutilated and slain with blades called pangas, normally used for harvesting crops by hand. Also during the 1990s, bloody ethnic conflicts in Bosnia and other parts of the former Eastern European nation of Yugoslavia left thousands dead.

▲ Members of the Argentine Forensic Anthropology Team at work in 2003 at a mass grave in a cemetery in Argentina. The one hundred people buried there were probably political prisoners killed during a former dictatorship.

These crimes against humanity cannot be properly investigated or judged without the evidence provided by forensic anthropologists. For that evidence to be useful, it must be collected in a systematic way. When a mass grave is opened, before any of the remains are touched, the excavators photograph and map the site. Then each body is photographed just as it is found, carefully placed in a body bag, and removed. Later, each set of remains will be measured and photographed again, with special attention to details that might help with identification, such as tattoos or clothing.

Mass graves pose special challenges to forensic investigators. Body parts may become detached and intermingled, making it hard to place finger and toe bones, for example, with the bodies to which they belong. In addition, when bodies are packed together in close contact without wrappings, DNA can be transferred from one corpse to another through skin contact or by means of seeping fluids. Investigators who are using DNA tests to identify the dead must obtain uncontaminated samples, such as tissue from muscles or internal organs.

One of the biggest tasks facing the excavators of a mass grave is gathering information to identify the buried victims. This means collecting dental and medical records, X rays, and photographs, if these are

▲ British forensic anthropologist Kerry-Ann Martin was one of many specialists who helped identify remains from mass graves in the former nation of Yugoslavia, where ethnic and political violence led to large-scale massacres during the 1990s.

available, for all missing people who may have been placed in the mass grave. The help of surviving family members is vital in this process. Family members are also asked to contribute DNA samples to be matched against samples taken from the bodies. Each recovered body must then be painstakingly examined according to the procedures of forensic anthropology, and the results of each examination recorded.

Investigating genocides is forensic anthropology on a scale that is horrifyingly large; it is difficult and demanding work that requires months or years of dedication. In the early 2000s, for example, forensic scientists spent five years identifying most of the seven thousand bodies recovered from a single mass grave in Bosnia. The men and women who patiently and carefully exhume hundreds of decomposing bodies from a single grave, then work for weeks and months to identify as many of the dead as possible, are truly serving all humanity.

▶ MURDER MOST FOUL

By 1998 neighbors had noticed that a house in the city of Poughkeepsie, New York, was giving off a terrible odor. The police noticed the odor, too, when they came to the house to interview Kendall Francois, who lived there with his parents and younger sister. Francois had been arrested a few years earlier for beating up a local woman who worked as a prostitute, and police wanted to talk to him now in connection with their investigation of the unexplained disappearances from the area of six women in less than two years. But nothing about Francois made the police suspicious. They did mention, in their report of the visit to his house, that the place was littered with garbage and smelled awful.

The reason for the dreadful smell became all too clear when police returned to the house after being told by a woman that Francois had tried to kill her. This time officers arrested Francois and made a thorough search of the residence.

Forensic anthropologist Robert Mann of CIL has called the Francois residence "a house of horrors." It contained the remains of eight murdered women. Francois had buried three of the bodies under the house. He had dismembered the other five and stored them in the attic. Although the body parts were mostly skeletonized, decomposing tissue still clung to some of the bones.

A medical examiner for the New York State Police, Barbara Wolf, realized that the body parts of five women were jumbled together and asked Mann to help with the challenge of reassembling them. Wolf's request was important for several reasons. Authorities wanted to know if all of the eight victims' body parts were present—and they also wanted to know if *more* than eight victims were represented. In addition, authorities hoped to return complete remains to the victims' families for burial.

Identifying the eight victims from their skulls was not difficult. Dental records of the missing women were available, and the forensic examiners could compare these records to the victims' teeth. Putting the severed arms, legs, and torsos of the five dismembered women back together with the right skulls would be much harder. Mann said it was like "trying to distinguish the pieces from five jigsaw puzzles when all the pieces had been mixed together in one box."

All Francois's victims were white women of roughly the same general body size. This meant that there were few obvious clues to tell examiners which body parts belonged to which victim. The examiners had to rely on painstaking measurements and careful comparisons. Because the bodies had been cut apart in slightly different ways, the examiners were finally able to fit all the pieces together. Cut marks on the women's bones showed that Francois had used a hacksaw on the bodies. The use of a saw to dismember crime victims is not unusual, sadly. Francois's cut marks were unusual, however. The marks revealed that the killer had sawn only partway through each bone, then snapped the bone to break it. This created distinctive jagged ends on the bones, which helped the examiners match up the pieces that belonged together.

Francois was convicted of eight counts of first-degree murder and imprisoned for life. Despite the savagery of his crimes and the gruesome mutilations of his victims, the investigators had carried out a successful forensic analysis. Every day across the United

States and the world, forensic anthropologists bring order and insight to the messy aftermath of murder, mystery, and mayhem. Whether they are identifying a single bone from an unknown source or sorting out the victims of a mass crime, forensic anthropologists use their knowledge and skill to read the evidence of the bones.

▼ GLOSSARY

anthropology the study of human beings past and present, with emphasis on the differences among groups

anthropometry measuring the human body; the database of knowledge gained from measuring many bodies is called anthropometrics

autopsy a medical examination performed on a body to find the cause of death; a forensic autopsy also tries to establish the time and manner of death

coroner public official responsible for determining cause of death; the position does not require medical training

criminalistics the study of physical evidence from a crime scene

criminology the study of crime, criminals, and criminal behavior

decomposition the process of decay and tissue breakdown that happens after death as a result of the action of bacteria

entomology the study of insects; forensic entomology uses knowledge of insects and observations of their behavior in crime investigation

facial reconstruction building up a portrait of a person based on skull measurements; may be done with computer software, with a three-dimensional model, or in sketch form

forensic science the use of scientific knowledge or methods to investigate crimes, identify suspects, and try criminal cases in court

forensics in general, debate or review of any question of fact relating to the law; often used to refer to forensic science

genocide deliberate attempt to eliminate an entire racial, ethnic, or religious group by killing all its members

homicide murder

maggots insect larvae; in the context of forensics, the insects are species that feed and breed on human remains

medical examiner (ME) public official responsible for determining cause of death; the position requires medical training

odontology the study of teeth and dental work; forensic odontology is the use of teeth to identify the dead

osteology the study of the skeleton and of bone

pathologist physician who specializes in the study of illness and death, especially in determining the cause of death

postmortem after death

postmortem interval (PMI) the amount of time between death and the finding of the body

prosecutor attorney who argues the case against an accused criminal and acts on behalf of either the people of a state or the federal government

skeletonized consisting mostly or entirely of bones, with little or no soft tissue remaining

taphonomy the study of the series of changes that take place in a body after death

toxicology the branch of medical and forensic science that deals with drugs, poisons, and other harmful substances

▼ FIND OUT MORE

FURTHER READING

Adams, Bradley J. *Forensic Anthropology.* New York: Chelsea House, 2006.

Denega, Danielle. *Skulls and Skeletons: True-Life Stories of Bone Detectives.* New York: Franklin Watts, 2007.

Ferllini, Roxana. *Silent Witness: How Forensic Anthropology Is Used to Solve the World's Toughest Crimes.* Willowdale, Ont.: Firefly, 2002.

Funkhluser, John. *Forensic Science for High School Students.* Dubuque, IA: Kendall Hunt, 2005.

Libal, Angela. *Forensic Anthropology.* Broomall, PA: Mason Crest: 2005.

Mattern, Joanne. *Forensics.* San Diego, CA: Blackbirch Press, 2004.

Platt, Richard. *Crime Scene: The Ultimate Guide to Forensic Science.* New York: Dorling Kindersley, 2003.

Shone, Rob. *Corpses and Skeletons: The Science of Forensic Anthropology.* New York: Rosen, 2008.

Thomas, Peggy. *Forensic Anthropology: The Growing Science of Talking Bones.* Rev. ed. New York: Facts On File, 2003.

WEBSITES

http://web.utk.edu/~fac/
The Forensic Anthropology Center of the University of Tennessee, home of the famous Body Farm, offers insights into the practice of forensic anthropology on its web page.

www.theabfa.org/index.html

The American Board of Forensic Anthropology (ABFA) offers information about its program for becoming a certified forensic anthropologist.

www.aafs.org/yfsf/index.htm

The website of the American Academy of Forensic Sciences features the Young Forensic Scientists Forum, with information on careers in forensics. The site also links to other Internet resources.

www.jpac.pacom.mil/index.php?page=home&size=100&ind=0

The JPAC site gives an overview of this military department's mission to identify and repatriate the remains of missing American service people. A section on the Central Identification Laboratory discusses the role of forensic anthropologists in this effort.

www.crimezzz.net/forensic_history/index.htm

The Crimeline page offers a brief timeline of developments in forensic science from prehistory to the present.

www.forensicmag.com/

Forensic Magazine's web page features case studies and news about developments in forensic anthropology and other branches of forensic science.

▼ BIBLIOGRAPHY

The author found these books and articles especially helpful when researching this volume.

Bass, Bill, and Jon Jefferson. *Beyond the Body Farm*. New York: Morrow, 2007.

Davis, Matthew, and Susan Halla-Borelli. "What Anthropology Brings to the Table." *Forensic Magazine*, December 2008–January 2009, online at www.forensicmag.com/articles.asp?pid=239

Hunter, John, and Margaret Cox. *Forensic Archaeology: Advances in Theory and Practice*. London and New York: Routledge, 2005.

Jackson, Charles. "Forensic Art Defined and Explained." *Forensic Magazine*, Winter 2004, online at www.forensicmag.com/articles.asp?pid=24

Jervis, Rick. "Forensics Lab Brings Bold Cases back to Life." *USA Today*, February 26, 2009, online at www.usatoday.com/tech/science/2009-02-26-forensics_N.htm

Klepinger, Linda L. *Fundamentals of Forensic Anthropology*. Hoboken, NJ: Wiley, 2006.

Mann, Robert, and Miryam Ehrlich Williamson. *Forensic Detective*. New York: Ballantine, 2006.

Maples, William R., and Michael Browning. *Dead Men Do Tell Tales*. New York: Doubleday, 1994.

Nafte, Myriam. *Flesh and Bone: An Introduction to Forensic Anthropology*. Durham, NC: Carolina Academic Press, 2000.

Rhine, Stanley. *Bone Voyage: A Journey in Forensic Anthropology*. Albuquerque: University of New Mexico Press, 1998.

▼ INDEX

▼ ABOUT THE AUTHOR

REBECCA STEFOFF is the author of many books on scientific subjects for young readers. In addition to writing previous volumes in the Forensic Science Investigated series, she has explored the world of evolutionary biology in Marshall Cavendish's Family Trees series; she also wrote *Robot* and *Camera* for Marshall Cavendish's Great Inventions series. After publishing *Charles Darwin and the Evolution Revolution* (Oxford University Press, 1996), she appeared in the *A&E Biography* program on Darwin and his work. Stefoff lives in Portland, Oregon. You can learn more about her books for young readers at **www.rebeccastefoff.com**.